Personal Statements

How to write a UCAS
Personal Statement

Paul Telfer

Acknowledgements

The publishers would like to thank all those who agreed to the publication of their statements and take the opportunity of wishing them every success with their chosen degrees and future careers.

About the author

Paul Telfer is a teacher with over 20 years' experience of advising and guiding sixth-formers through their Personal Statements. He is also an award-winning playwright and television writer.

Published by iris books
PO BOX 136
Thirsk
North Yorkshire
Y07 2WU

ISBN 978-0-9519284-1-4
Editor: Sharon Telfer
Design by Adkins Design

Contents

How to use this book

The purpose of this book is to give you confidence and certainty – to allow you to write your UCAS Personal Statement with the minimum of assistance.

For this reason it gives you a precise outline to follow.

It sets out a step-by-step process that allows you to build a full and structured statement.

The simple structure is outlined on page 16.

It also shows you how to improve your phrasing and sentence structure and achieve an appropriate tone of voice.

It shows how to make your Personal Statement interesting: and, in turn, to make you interesting to Admissions Tutors.

As you work your way through the structure, you will also meet a series of

rules of thumb

Follow the rules of thumb throughout the process. These rules are listed opposite, and then appear in the book as each rule becomes specifically relevant. They are there to help you.

rules of thumb

- be specific
- **start early**
- start by using 5 sections
- be enthusiastic
- **tell them something about you**
- avoid obvious statement and cliché
- imply rather than state
- redraft
- prepare for interview
- show your subject means something beyond the classroom
- demonstrate maturity
- **always keep your chosen course in mind**
- **end sentences and paragraphs with nouns**
- don't ignore out of school or college activities
- aim for a circular structure
- **construct bridges**
- leave for a couple of days before redrafting
- avoid passive writing
- use a variety of punctuation
- stick to what you know
- include your own ideas

ALWAYS REMEMBER THE ONE GOLDEN RULE:

be specific

What is UCAS?

UCAS stands for University and Colleges Admissions Service.

UCAS is the central organisation that processes applications for full-time undergraduate courses at UK universities and colleges. Each year it handles more than 350,000 applications. UCAS passes on your details to your selected universities and standardises the application process.

UCAS ensures that you do not arrive to study your degree and find yourself a victim of double booking.

On your UCAS form, you will list your GCSE results and your sixth form will predict your final exam grades. Your college or school will also give you a reference recommending your suitability for your chosen course. These three areas are vitally important.

You are then given the opportunity of writing your own reference – your Personal Statement – an online document of 4,000 characters including spaces that will persuade your chosen university that you should study the degree of your choice at their institution.

UCAS forwards this information to your chosen universities and their Admissions Tutors make a decision on your future.

For further information on UCAS and admissions see their website: www.ucas.com.

What is a UCAS Personal Statement?

The UCAS Personal Statement is possibly the single most important document that you will ever write.

In an increasingly competitive world, the statement is your chance to impress: it is a letter, job application, CV and interview all in one.

ITS FUNDAMENTAL PURPOSE IS TO SHOW UNIVERSITIES

'what makes you tick' ...and control the next step of your future.

How do universities use the statement?

Your statement has three principal uses:

■ When university Admissions Tutors read your statement, it helps them decide whether to offer you a place on your chosen course.

■ Where relevant, it may convince the university to call you for an interview. It helps the universities decide what questions to ask you at interview – and enables you to shape the questions they ask.

■ Your exam results may not fulfil the university's conditional offer – the grades they expect you to attain to achieve a place on their course. In this event, Admissions Tutors will study the statement again and re-evaluate your worth.

Your college reference and your Personal Statement may then convince them that you are worth a place.

What information is most useful to the university?

Your fundamental aim is to demonstrate to the universities that you really want to study their course.

Universities like to see that you have already begun to devote yourself to a serious experience of your chosen field.

You need to inform them of academic or wider qualifications and work and life experience that is relevant to your chosen course.

Experience of the wider community is useful, and your statement must display maturity:

maturity = dependability

demonstrate maturity

It can be helpful to write about your aims – what you hope to gain from the course.

Any long-term career plans may be interesting, but their significance can depend on the department and the university – Admissions Tutors hold a variety of different views on the importance of career plans. For this reason it is best to refer to them briefly.

What must your statement convey?

You must use your statement to make the best impression on Admissions Tutors. To do this you must:

- Show your motivation.

- Show genuine enthusiasm for your chosen course.

- Show your academic enthusiasm.

  Hopefully, you have already demonstrated this to your school or college and the enthusiasm for your chosen course will also be clearly evident in the school's reference.

- Show more than the purely academic. Universities want to know what kind of person you are.

- Show Admissions Tutors insights into your personality, interests, achievement and relevant work experience.

- Show that you are a well-rounded individual. Paint a fuller picture of yourself. You may be called for interview and the statement will play an important part in this decision. It will certainly play a part in the interviewer's selection of questions.

When to start?

The annual opening date is 1 September.

Entries for Oxford and Cambridge, and for Medicine, Dentistry and Veterinary Medicine must be in by 15 October. (See page 64 for important dates.)

Writing your statement should take you three weeks to a month. Don't leave writing your statement to the last minute. Allow yourself a month for proper preparation and redrafting.

start early

By applying early you remove considerable pressure from yourself, allowing you to concentrate on your studies.

It's never too early

Ideally, you should be aware of this document in Year 11 – aged 15 – even if this is merely to consider various possible career routes and course choices. At this stage, you should begin to think about the kind of information your statement requires.

You should become aware of what is specifically required as you enter the sixth form or sixth form college – Year 12. By the end of that year, you should have done your best to research courses and the universities that can give you what you want from life. It is then up to you to persuade them that they need you.

You need to impress them: they are investing in you.

Remember: you are introducing yourself to the university and department that will shape the rest of your life. You are in competition for places.

Your statement must make you interesting.

Where can it go wrong?

The Personal Statement is often the weakest and most poorly considered section of the UCAS application. This can be hugely disappointing to the universities – and totally detrimental to your chances of gaining an offer.

Signs of a bad statement

Given the importance of the statement, the most irritating and annoying weakness is downright sloppiness.

- **Waffle and lack of structure.** Your Personal Statement must be planned, logical and as clear as possible. Too many weak applicants don't know what to write or have no sense of ordered planning.

- **Sloppy presentation and content.** Weak applicants misjudge the tone of their statement: you are writing a serious and professional job application.

- **Too short.** Make the most of the space available: being too brief might make you sound uninteresting. But don't forget that you have only 4,000 characters including spaces.

- **Dullness.** As a prospective undergraduate your statement must demonstrate that you are interesting – and extremely interested and enthusiastic about your chosen course.

■ **Underselling.** Don't hide your light under a bushel. Admissions Tutors like to see somebody with a well-rounded personality and interests: achievements beyond the academic are important.

■ **Poor grammar and spelling.** Checking spelling is essential. Get people to check your statement. Admissions Tutors will assume it to be your best work.

■ **Lies.** Remember that your Personal Statement will be referred to if called for interview. You must be certain that all your claims are genuine.

■ **Generalising.** Give your statement depth. For example, don't say simply that you are interested in music, state what particular music you prefer and why.

■ **Plagiarism.** Don't be tempted to copy other people's statements. UCAS have invested a considerable amount of money in procedures to identify plagiarised material. And, apart from the dubious morality of such practice, plagiarism is rarely effective, tending to make your statement sound shallow or false. Give your statement your identity.

The statements in this book are here as models for you to follow – not to copy.

Nearly all of these pitfalls can be avoided by remembering the principle rule of thumb.

REMEMBER THE GOLDEN RULE:

be specific

Making the right start

Before you begin to think about yourself, you should find out as much as possible about your chosen course.

Research the type of course that universities offer in your chosen subject. There is an increasing amount of information on university websites, and you should also consult Brian Heap's *Degree Course Offers* (published by Trotman). The UCAS website is a useful starting place if you want to find this and similar books. When you feel you fully understand the course you are applying to you can begin to consider your statement.

However, before you begin the essential process of structuring your statement, start with a simple list.

Opening list

This is straightforward: list everything positive that makes you who you are – a list of all your qualities. Remember the Admissions Tutor is interested in you. He or she wants to know who you are: what makes you tick. So, even in this early note form:

On page 74, you will find a completed statement for Veterinary Science; this was that applicant's original list.

- How long have I wanted to be a vet?
- Results – successful AS results
- Subjects I really like
- Aspects of those subjects that I really like
- Wider reading

- ■ Work experience
  - ■ Oaklands Surgery
  - ■ Kebir Surgery
  - ■ Lambing
  - ■ Abattoir
  - ■ Farrier
  - ■ Farmwork
- ■ Teaching and work
- ■ Riding, eventing
- ■ Riding captain – team organisation
- ■ Sport – school teams
- ■ Sport out of school
- ■ Social activities
- ■ Prefect
- ■ Bronze/Silver/Gold D of E
- ■ Young Enterprise
- ■ Debating – national competition
- ■ Drama – school plays, local drama society

This is his list. Yours will be different. You will use some of the points on your list, and you will abandon others, but the list serves as your starting point. What makes the statement difficult is that you have to take these points and work them into a comprehensive prose account of who you are.

Follow the steps described. Don't be tempted to skip a section.

Save all your work as Word documents. You can then easily transfer your final statement to the UCAS electronic site.

Now turn your attention to structure. This could not be easier to follow.

The five-section structure

Structure is the area that the majority of applicants find most difficult. It needn't be if you follow the five-section structure.

start by using 5 sections

1 Why
Why have you chosen this course?

2 What
What have you done to demonstrate your passionate interest in the course subject?

3 Academic
How do your AS and A2 or other academic subjects relate to your chosen course?

4 Interests – activities and sport
What have you learned from your activities that is relevant to your chosen course and university life?

5 Conclusion
What personal experience or ambitions can you link to your chosen course to give the statement a sense of completion?

Section 1: Why?

In this section you need to state why you have chosen your prospective course.

This opening paragraph may be the shortest of the statement, but it is the one that must grab the reader's interest.

be enthusiastic

Admissions Tutors want students to enthuse about their chosen course.

You must demonstrate that you have thought thoroughly about the suitability of the course and that you understand what particular courses are offering. Show the Admissions Tutor that this is the course for you.

First sentences

The opening lines of any piece of writing are vitally important – poems, novels, films, pop songs – your statement is no different.

Your opening sentence will arguably be the most important that you write, so clearly you will need to give it a great deal of thought. You are unlikely to find the best words in your first draft – and you will be very lucky if you write the opening section of your statement in five minutes. You are beginning a long process and you will need patience if you are to get things right.

Initially, you may benefit from a step-by-step approach.

On its website (www.ucas.com), UCAS suggests that your first step should be to write out the reasons why you are applying to your chosen course. These might be such things as:

- You enjoy the subject.

- You enjoy particular aspects of the subject.

- You look forward to studying it in greater depth.

- Your work experience confirmed your interest.

- You look forward to putting theory into practice.

- You possess the skills required for the course.

- You have a particular career in mind or particular plans for after your degree.

The UCAS website also suggests some starter sentences for your statement. Sentences such as…

> "Success and interest in AS level Chemistry confirmed my interest in studying Chemistry."

…may help you get started on your first draft, but consider how many other applicants will be using similar sentences. You will need to end up with something more individual if your statement is to make an impact.

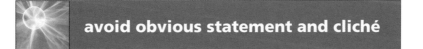

tell them something about you

Remember, opening sentences establish the tone of your statement. It is important to give your statement your identity and vital that you demonstrate enthusiasm.

For this reason you should try to:

avoid obvious statement and cliché

> "I have always been passionate about Economics…"

> "Languages fascinate me…"

Such starter sentences sound reasonable enough, but thousands of applicants begin their statement in this predictable way. Using one of these clichés may help get you started. However, at some stage you should redraft and make your sentence individual.

There are various ways to do this.

Implication

Imply your passionate interest in your chosen course.

imply rather than state

Rather than stating your passion or fascination, make the Admissions Tutor aware that you are passionate or fascinated. To do this, you need to use specific examples.

REMEMBER THE GOLDEN RULE:

be specific

In your opening paragraph, try to find something that is specific to you – a particular area that associates you with the subject.

The examples below suggest what you should be aiming to achieve in your final statement. There are a number of ways of approaching this.

APPROACH 1

Begin with a very brief anecdote from personal experience.

ENGINEERING

> "Since dismantling my first toys at an early age, I have been compelled to discover how and why things work."

ENGLISH LITERATURE

> "Even before I could read I loved books! My parents were always reading to me and I am fortunate to have listened to thousands of hours of 'talking books'; this may have been when I first fell in love with the sound of words."

APPROACH 2

Begin with a specific element of the subject that appeals to you.

ENGINEERING

> "It is the engineer's ability to turn theory into reality that interests me. I want to learn about how systems can be designed and controlled."

COMPUTING

> "I want to be at the forefront of the radical innovation and development that will transform and enhance our lives."

APPROACH 3

Refer to an expert in the field, for example, an author who you have found particularly inspiring.

PSYCHOLOGY

> "Gitta Sereny's 'Cries Unheard' first stimulated my awareness of Psychology."

APPROACH 4

Refer to something specific from your life experience that led to your interest in your chosen course.

COMPUTING

> "When I was fourteen, my personal website gained second place in the Yell International Youth Web Site of the Year – being beaten only by the BBC for the top award."

ECONOMICS

> "Childhood in a developing Ghanaian economy demonstrated firsthand the dreadful human consequences of poverty and social deprivation."

By being specific in this way, your enthusiasm is immediately apparent. Therefore, you can avoid such obvious statement and cliché as:

> "I have always been passionate about…"

In these examples the candidates' passionate interest and involvement in the chosen subject are clearly implied rather than stated. Their enthusiasm is so obvious that it doesn't need stating.

You should endeavour to use this technique of implication throughout your statement. Ideally, let the Admissions Tutor become aware of your enthusiastic commitment without having to tell him or her that it exists.

imply rather than state

You should be aiming to match the tone of the examples above. Not everyone will find this easy and you are highly unlikely to express yourself so successfully in your first draft. It is unlikely that the applicants above wrote these sentences in their first or even second draft. You must be patient.

With patience and hard work you can achieve a similar standard.

Sometimes it is a good idea to write the rest of the statement and then come back to the opening sentence.

This way you may be able to link to something that you say in the conclusion – or by that stage everything may simply seem a great deal easier.

Make your first sentence personal. Tell them something specific about yourself.

be specific

This technique allows the Admissions Tutor to gain an immediate sense of your personality – what makes you tick.

Opening paragraphs

Having written your first sentence or two, you should now write your opening paragraph, making the Admissions Tutor aware of your enthusiasm – demonstrating that this course is the course for you.

What exactly inspires you about your chosen course? Ask yourself the following:

- **Why** do you enjoy the subject?

- **Which** particular aspects do you enjoy?

- **What** specific interests would you like to explore in greater depth?

- **What** theories in particular would you enjoy putting into practice?

- **Which** skills do you possess?

- **How** did work experience help?

Ultimately, you may decide that you do not need to address all of these questions in the final draft of your statement – but these are the kind of questions that you must ask yourself in your initial draft.

Remember: what you write now is not set in stone.

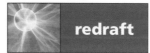
redraft

Don't be afraid of writing a phrase, a sentence or a paragraph again. The statement must have your identity: don't be afraid to change things as you get more confident.

Here is an example of an excellent opening:

> "Even before I fully understood what they were, rocks, minerals, fossils and gemstones had a compelling fascination. I was attracted by their vivid colours and amazed by the ages of the specimens that I found and bought. But it was when I became intellectually curious – intrigued by the manner of their formation – that my obsession with Geology really began."

This paragraph has been redrafted and polished to get to this stage. Remember, your final opening paragraph is highly unlikely to be the first one that you write.

However, you need something to get you started. So write an opening paragraph first and then come back and polish in your second draft.

Preparing for interview

Before you begin Section 2, it is worth pausing to think about interview preparation.

Not everyone will be called to interview. However, if your course is highly competitive or you are applying to a particularly prestigious university, then it is highly likely that you will be interviewed.

Whether you consider it likely or not, it is a good idea to assume that you will be called for interview. If you assume that someone may question you on your claims and experiences, it will focus the mind – and give your statement a more genuine and sincere tone.

prepare for interview

It is pointless lying about your experience. Genuine claims have the ring of authenticity and capture your true nature.

Remember the purpose of the statement is to demonstrate what makes you tick. Make sure that you are writing about areas that hold a genuine interest. Let Admissions Tutors know what you want to talk about.

Admissions Tutors and interviewers will assume that you have mentioned something in your statement because it is significant to you. Refer to it in your statement because you would be happy to talk about it.

always keep your chosen course in mind

Section 2: What?

In your second section show what you have done to demonstrate your enthusiastic interest in your chosen subject. What relevant experience have you had?

This section really counts. Admissions Tutors scrutinise this section. If they haven't seen something worthwhile by the end of this section, they may read no further.

If you do not impress in Section 2, your statement is likely to go on the reject pile.

You should begin by referring directly to your subject. In the second part of this section you can include general demonstrations of your enthusiasm – for example, relevant work experience.

Academic experience

This is your opportunity to demonstrate that you have a mature interest in your chosen subject and academic study generally. You should aim to show that your academic experience has urged you to discover more.

Try to take it further than the syllabus you are studying.

 show your subject means something beyond the classroom

Demonstrate that your knowledge of the subject has convinced you that you will enjoy a degree in the subject – and be successful. You should also persuade the Admissions Tutor that you have some idea of the academic rigours of your future course.

REMEMBER THE GOLDEN RULE:
be specific

Let them know that you have a genuine academic curiosity by referring to specific areas of the subject that you are interested in.

For example, if applying for English, don't just say that you have enjoyed the course, say that you have enjoyed specific areas.

Don't merely say:

> "I really enjoyed studying Shakespeare…"

Think specifically...

> "I enjoyed 'Hamlet' and 'A Midsummer Night's Dream'."

And then think specifically again...

> "I responded to Hamlet's psychological turmoil and the pure theatricality of 'A Midsummer Night's Dream'."

Your specific responses give the statement your identity. If you are specific, the statement will begin to sound like you, rather than a hundred other candidates.

Show that you have a love of your subject.

Be certain to make genuine claims: remember that part of the purpose of this section is to prepare the way for any interviews.

If you refer to specific subject areas, your interviewer is likely to ask you questions about those areas.

Taking our example above: if you say that you responded to Hamlet's psychological turmoil, the interviewer is likely to ask – "So. What did you find so fascinating about Hamlet's psychological turmoil?".

This approach allows you to talk about subject areas of specific interest. On the other hand, remember that you will look foolish if you cannot answer.

By all means begin with something that is part of your experience of A-level studies, but then take it a stage further. In this way, you appear both more interesting and enthusiastic.

ENGLISH LITERATURE

> "Having been inspired by the AS syllabus, I have attempted to broaden my experience of different eras and genres of literature – from 'The Battle of Maldon' and medieval works, such as the magical 'Gawain and the Green Knight', through to a particular love of 20th Century literature."

Be specific about your reading and then, as in the following examples, show that you have learnt from it.

PSYCHOLOGY

> "'Mind Watching – Why we Behave the Way we Do' by Hans and Michael Eysenk helped me gain a deeper understanding of topics such as mental illness. Both books made me aware of the significance of diagnostic labels, particularly when they cause people to systematically re-interpret all aspects of a patient's behaviour as symptomatic of the disorder they have been labelled with."

It is not just **wider reading** that can demonstrate your genuine depth of interest in a subject.

Courses and **conferences** demonstrate that your interest is genuine.

VETERINARY SCIENCE

> "I attended two residential courses at the University of Nottingham, 'VetSix' and 'VetSim': sessions ranged from reptiles and exotics to suturing, keyhole surgery and emergency callout simulation, and I attended lectures on parasites, surgical techniques and holistic treatments. I found both courses intriguing and their diversity affirmed my desire to be a vet."

GEOLOGY

> "When I was fourteen, I attended Scottish Geology Week, a fascinating five days of geological discovery: an inspection of Arthur's Seat; a visit to the BGS in Edinburgh; a view of the cretaceous-tertiary boundary; and a quest for Grapholites in Dobbs Lynn were highlights of a totally compelling five days."

Notice how each candidate's passion for his subject is obvious without being stated.

In each of the three examples above, the candidates' experience demonstrates the value of starting early. Not everyone knows what they want to do by the age of 15, but these days it helps. It increases your relevant experience and gives your statement an air of essential maturity.

demonstrate maturity

Remember the importance of maturity. The Admissions Tutors are looking for students they can trust.

Relevant work experience

Clearly, relevant work experience can demonstrate certain qualities required by particular courses. However, avoid talking about work experience just for the sake of it. Give your work experience a purpose.

You might begin by writing a list of duties or responsibilities experienced through work and then match them to skills that you learned from those duties.

Some of the mature skills that you might demonstrate in this section are:

- Communication
- Computer literacy
- Diplomacy
- Independence
- Initiative
- Listening

- Management

- Persuasion

- Problem solving

- Teamwork

- Working to deadlines

Look to incorporate relevant words from this list into this section. However, don't list more than three. Choose the three qualities that you consider **most relevant to your particular course.**

always keep your chosen course in mind

When you have your list, you know what you want to say and can begin to write your second section.

Work experience allows you to demonstrate the skills that you have developed as a result of your experience. These are often vital skills – skills that impress Admissions Tutors because they demonstrate maturity and a willingness to go that extra distance beyond the classroom.

be specific

Here's another example from a successful candidate:

COMPUTING

> "…this led to six weeks' employment at Uniqma as a 'student consultant'. Here I learned about the importance of teamwork and the meeting of deadlines. I was involved in all computer aspects of the company, including problem solving with databases, modelling spreadsheets and raising levels of computer awareness and efficiency throughout the company. I learned a tremendous amount about working with people and met new experiences in the field of computing that served to convince me that computing was my future…"

This applicant relates his specific learning to his specific experience particularly well.

always keep your chosen course in mind

In Section 2 make work experience directly relevant to your proposed course.

Remember that the length of this work-experience part of your second section will depend on the type of degree that you are applying for. With a three-year academic course, such as English Literature or Physics, there is little that can be added in terms of work experience. However, if applying for a sandwich or vocational degree you will need to be writing fairly substantially.

Vocational courses

With good reason, tutors for vocational courses expect prospective undergraduates to have demonstrated specific interest in their chosen career. If you want to be a medic, a barrister or a vet then it is essential to demonstrate that you have explored the area and have firsthand experience and knowledge of your chosen career.

By the time you write your statement, you should have relevant firsthand experience.

Such experience demonstrates a passionate interest – an interest that goes beyond the confines of the syllabus and classroom.

The following examples look at medicine. However, the methods these candidates adopt in discussing their work experience could be applied to other vocational subjects.

Medicine

It is particularly important to demonstrate awareness of the demands of medicine beyond your academic syllabus.

Medical schools are incredibly competitive. It is not uncommon for applicants predicted to achieve three grade As to be rejected by all their chosen universities. The universities need to be able to differentiate. **For medics this section of the statement is vital.**

The two examples that follow demonstrate the kind of specific detail required for a successful section – but which do you consider to be the best and why?

STATEMENT A

"Over the last three years, I have thoroughly enjoyed gaining an insight into Medicine and important aspects of the profession. Over the summer holidays I spent a week in a GP surgery and a further memorable week in Hartlepool General Hospital. In the surgery, I shadowed and observed four GPs giving me an insight into primary healthcare; I was impressed and engaged by the diagnosis process from common colds to a rare case of Lymes Disease! Hospital provided me with an insight into specialist areas of medicine. I shadowed two paediatricians, a child psychiatrist and observed a diabetic clinic. Here I became aware of the numerous psychological hurdles that accompany the treatment of adolescent diabetics. In the Intensive Care Unit, I was fascinated by such life-saving devices as the defibrillator, intravenous drip and the ECG monitoring new born babies in the Post Natal Unit. One aspect I would particularly enjoy would be working in a team."

STATEMENT B

"To help me gain insight into the world of medicine, I spent three weeks on work experience placements during the summer holidays. I worked in the Accident and Emergency Department in North Tees Hospital, in the Intensive Care Unit at Middlesbrough General and in a General Practitioners' Surgery in Thornaby. At the A&E Department, I observed nurses performing triage and how they extracted vital information about a patient's history. I shadowed doctors into treatment rooms, observed a variety of interesting lacerations and fractures and witnessed the removal of several foreign bodies! I particularly enjoyed looking at X-rays as the doctor would explain what they were looking for and what the X-ray showed. It was amazing how much information could be extracted from an X-ray – and how tiny some of the clues were! The Intensive Care Unit showed me a very different side of medicine. I observed a tracheostomy and a muscle biopsy. I was privileged to join the ward rounds each morning and worked closely with the consultant anaesthetist who explained how the life maintaining equipment operated and how each patient was being treated. Working at the Medical Centre showed me how vital team work is to the profession. The GP I shadowed at the

> surgery also worked at the hospital and I was able to observe him performing colonoscopies and gastroscopies as well as the removal of various cysts and ulcers."

Both applicants are now at medical school: one at St Andrew's and one at Cambridge.

Their **enthusiasm** and **work ethic** shines. They have spent many weeks and months working to fulfil their ambitions. They also spent many hours perfecting their statement.

- Each applicant began by making a list of their relevant medical experience.

- They then paired their experience with the knowledge, understanding and insight they had gained.

- Their next step was to write about their experience in fluent sentences.

- They then completed the rest of their statement, returning to this section in their later drafts to improve their phrasing and communication.

Never be afraid of redrafting.

This book shows you the standard you should aim to achieve: it is highly unlikely that you will produce paragraphs of this standard in your first draft. But you must aspire to something similar to be offered a place to study a subject such as Medicine.

Each of these medical applications was subject to a rigorous redrafting process. Their final sections would have undergone *at least* five drafts before reaching the level that you have just read.

So which do you consider the better section?

The question is rather unfair. As both students are now studying at their first-choice universities, both statements were clearly successful.

However, it should be clear that B is that bit better than A. It not only gives his medical experiences, **but discusses specifically what he has learnt from them**.

He has been specific about the exact duties/shadowing experiences and then explained the skills and knowledge acquired.

General vocational courses

Not everyone is applying for courses like Medicine where experience is vital. Work experience in a hospital will be directly relevant to a medical degree: for these applications, it's advisable that the section on work experience should be long and detailed.

However, for more general vocational courses, your work experience in Section 2 may read more like this:

BUSINESS STUDIES

"Work experience as a clerical assistant in a large supermarket enabled me to develop a number of important skills. Working in a small team ensured that I was able to **listen carefully** to others and **work co-operatively** with a variety of different people. In addition, at certain times I had to work **independently** which allowed me to use my own initiative. Such skills will prove extremely useful on my Business Studies degree."

The bold highlights are here to show you how the candidate has discussed the skills and knowledge acquired. The online application does not facilitate such presentational devices as bold or italics.

For another excellent illustration, look back at the computing example on page 28.

Other relevant experience

Our Geologist could not demonstrate his enthusiasm through work experience. But his heartfelt passion for Geology shines through a combination of academic and relevant, subject-based experience.

GEOLOGY

"As my secondary school did not offer Geology GCSE, I found a private tutor and we had two great years of one-to-one study. My coursework involved a study of faulting and folding; faulting at Staithes on the North Yorkshire coast and folding at Apes Tor in the Peak District – Geology takes you to such great places! My laboratory experiment investigated the different effects of acid rain on limestone and granite.

'Rock shops' have always lured me, and I have collected a wide variety of specimens. My current pride and joy is a section of a Brazilian Geode with spectacular amethyst crystals – closely followed by my precious malachite and onyx chess set. I have been a keen lapidarist since primary school and have a full range of equipment. My favourite labour of love is my large cross-sectioned ammonite with dog-tooth calcite crystals in all of its chambers.

My current original research project is a study of a quarry face section of the Cleveland Dyke near my home; I am also investigating the alignment of phenocrysts and the degree of metamorphism in the host rocks – mainly shale. I also intend to return to Staithes and complete my study on faulting."

Through his specific subject experience, our candidate shows that Geology means something to him. His Section 2 resonates with a geological understanding similar to the work experience of the two medics.

In the same way that the medics imply their enthusiasm for their subject, this candidate uses Section 2 to show that Geology makes him tick.

He has clearly gone beyond the syllabus. Not only does he demonstrate in-depth knowledge of his chosen subject, but he also gives an insight into his personality.

Notice that all three statements incorporate some subject-specific vocabulary. This reinforces their firsthand knowledge of their chosen subject.

Section 3: Academic

In your third section relate your chosen course to your full range of studies – your other AS and A2 subjects.

When you introduce your other AS and A2 subjects, it is a good idea to find a bridge from your principal subject into your secondary ones. The bold highlighting in the examples below shows you how candidates use this bridging device. Remember, you cannot use bold in your online application.

ENGLISH LITERATURE 1

"I have particularly enjoyed the changing interpretations of the American dream in 'Gatsby', 'Catcher in the Rye' and 'The Virgin Suicides'. **I enjoy exploring such traditions, associations and influences in literature. I am studying Rimbaud and Baudelaire as part of an optional study in French** – exploring the parallels between the French and English Romantic movements."

ENGLISH LITERATURE 2

"To me there is much more to English than just its writing: the social and historical contexts of 'Animal Farm' or non-fiction such as 'Down and Out in Paris and London' provide individual perspectives to my understanding of History and Politics. **As such, my A-level studies have complemented each other**; reading about European Fascism, I can better understand the feelings of those subjected to it."

Find aspects of your other AS and A2 subjects that are relevant to your principal subject.

always keep your chosen course in mind

PSYCHOLOGY

"**Studying Biology alongside Psychology** has helped me understand the links between physiological and neurological systems and behaviour; for example, how reduced levels of serotonin contribute to the onset of Seasonal Affective Disorder."

TRAVEL AND TOURISM

"While studying for my A levels, my self-confidence and public speaking skills have improved tremendously from my **Theatre Studies** course. I have also developed the ability to interact with different nationalities while studying and **speaking German**."

ECONOMICS

"I have found the analytical processes taught me by my **A-level Maths** course to be invaluable when drawing conclusions from varied data. Project work has introduced me to the idea of simplifying complex problems into simple workable ideas – a skill which I have found to be vitally important in the study of **Economics**."

MEDICINE

"**Studying Maths** has developed a logical way of thinking which is required for diagnostic medicine, **whilst Chemistry** has given me a solid foundation on which to build the physiology I will learn at medical school."

In all of these examples, the applicants find a link between their 'secondary' subjects and their chosen course subject.

Notice how each of the above paragraphs ends with a firm conclusion.

Journalists and screenwriters use a simple device to keep their readers involved to the end of a sentence. They end sentences and paragraphs with nouns. This gives a sense of finality to a sentence and contributes to the authoritative tone of your statement.

In other words, it helps you sound like you know what you are talking about in your statement.

end sentences and paragraphs with nouns

Your statement should now be taking shape.

Section 1 demonstrated why you want to study your chosen course.

Section 2 demonstrated what you have done to show your enthusiasm for your chosen course.

Section 3 related your other academic subjects to your chosen course.

You are now ready to tell Admissions Tutors a little more about you.

However, remember to keep your chosen course in mind even as you write about your activities and other interests in Section 4.

Section 4: Interests and activities

In your fourth section relate your school and college activities and general experience to your suitability for university.

Admissions Tutors need to know that you will survive university life and the rigours of a Higher Education course.

They need to know that you are capable of living and working independently.

Therefore this section of the statement must emphasise your maturity.

demonstrate maturity

Activities and interests – wider experiences – tend to indicate maturity. Maturity is one of the crucial qualities that Admissions Tutors trust and it will influence their decision.

Demonstrate **self-motivation**, **self-discipline** and **independence**. Show the Admissions Tutor a prospective undergraduate able to balance academic life with all the other pursuits which university life offers – sport, societies, acting, music...

Show the Admissions Tutor that you have what it takes to balance the various aspects of your life. Mention skills that show you are self-disciplined, self-motivated, hard-working, committed and able to build new friendships.

However, it's worth noting that a position of responsibility gained when you were young is less relevant than recent experiences.

Show that you are somebody who will benefit from life at university.

Remember that you are at university to study. Some students suffer because they do not get the balance right between work and social life. Your UCAS Personal Statement is definitely not the place to discuss your love of partying and nightclubs.

Universities do not want to give a valuable place to a candidate who drops out.

Show that you are a mature and interesting personality.

Though the number of mature students entering university increases annually, most of those applying for university are under twenty years of age. Even though you may consider yourself inexperienced, you should still demonstrate your maturity and willingness to seize opportunities.

Be honest about your experiences – but at the same time make the most of them. As stated earlier, your Personal Statement is not the place to hide your light under a bushel.

In Section 4, show the Admissions Tutor the general life skills you have learnt from your activities and address them to your course and general suitability for university life.

Explore how your interests and responsibilities may set you apart from many other students. As always:

Activity areas and matching skills

The following list is a good place to start.

Activity	Some relevant skills
Computer responsibilities	Organisation, reliability, trust
Debating society	Speaking and listening skills, teamwork, quick thinking
Drama production	Speaking and listening skills, teamwork, reliability, time management
Events organiser	Teamwork, time management, reliability
Form representative	Organisation, trust, people management
Library assistant	Trust, reliability
Musical concerts	Teamwork, reliability, discipline, time management
Musical instrument	Patience, determination, resolution
Prefect	Trust, dependability, teamwork
Voluntary work	Trust, selflessness, reliability

However, do not try and write about too many activities. If you have many to choose from, select those that are most relevant to your chosen subject.

Three activity areas would be ample: so if you have more choose your best three.

The examples below show the way that you should approach this section.

Describe your activity, then describe the skills that you have learnt. The highlighting emphasises where applicants have demonstrated skills learned. Remember: don't use highlighting in your statement.

> "Being nominated as a tutor group representative in the sixth form, provided me with the opportunity to **represent others** in a **responsible** and **fair manner**."

> "In addition, I have been involved in a number of drama productions as a technical assistant **working as part of a team** and ensuring that stage management kept to deadline."

> "A regular period of voluntary work with Help the Aged provided me with the opportunity to improve my **management** and **communication** skills."

"Being a member of the cast of 'Cabaret' was extremely rewarding. Acting has improved my **self-confidence** and **public speaking** skills. **I loved working in a team** and hope to be involved in more dramatic productions at university."

"Playing the violin to grade 7 and in the school orchestra has been extremely rewarding and **I learned to work in a team and be reliable.**"

"Speaking in front of a large audience as part of the Debating Society has been an excellent opportunity to develop my **public speaking** skills. I have taken part in a number of debates including the **regional final** of **The English Speaking Union Competition**. This experience has improved my **self-motivation** and **self-confidence**."

"As a library assistant my duties included **organising** the book loan system and stressed the importance of **punctuality** and **dependability**."

"The disco I arranged for the local hospice meant that I needed to be highly **organised**, **responsible** and totally **dependable**."

"My experience provided me with an excellent opportunity to work with people in a team whilst still demonstrating my **independence** and **self-motivation**."

Qualities and skills: useful terms

These are some of the skills – the nouns and adjectives – that you might refer to in this section.

- Approachable
- Communication
- Communicator
- Confidence/confident
- Diplomacy/diplomatic
- Dependability/dependable
- Efficiency/efficient
- Empathy/empathetic
- Helpfulness/helpful
- Independence/independent
- Initiative
- Listening
- Management

- Organisation/organised
- Problem solving
- Public speaking
- Punctuality/punctual
- Responsibility/responsible
- Self-expression
- Self-motivation/self-motivated
- Sensitivity/sensitive
- Teamwork
- Time management
- Trust/trustworthy
- Working to deadlines

Remember your purpose here.

By referring to these skills you are persuading the Admissions Tutor of your maturity. He or she needs to understand that you are capable of living and working independently.

It is not just your experiences at school or college that are important.

don't ignore out of school or college activities

The fact that you are prepared to pursue your interests beyond the school gates says a great deal about your motivation and reliability.

Interviewers may well ask you about some of these interests or experiences. They will gain a better view of what makes you tick, and you may feel more relaxed answering some non-academic questions.

Only write about genuine experiences – you may well be asked to talk at length about them should your offer depend on an interview.

In this section, as in all others, you must be specific.

So, identify and outline the key activities or experiences you have gained in a non-educational environment.

In no more than a sentence or two, outline some specific details about your pursuits. Then state why the experience is relevant to your application.

Try to find more than one activity that you enjoy and remember to tell the reader something about yourself. He or she will learn virtually nothing if your statement is too general.

If you are an avid reader, you might think something like this:

Initial thought:

> "I enjoy reading…"

To be more specific you might add another area:

> "I enjoy reading and the theatre…"

But here again, how many thousands of applicants could make the same claim?

Your claims will have a greater ring of authenticity and genuine interest if you are specific.

So, if you want to write about your interest in reading, ask yourself the following questions:

- What type of books do you enjoy?
- Which authors do you prefer?
- Why do you like these particular books?

In the activity section, wider reading does not need to be particularly academic. Depending on your course, you will have dealt with academic reading in Sections 2 and 3. Its purpose here is to show the Admissions Tutor something about you. For this reason it is best to suggest range or variety.

You might end up with something like:

> "Adventure books always kept me entertained. As a child I devoured Edgar Rice Burroughs and Rider Haggard. Nowadays, I enjoy novelists that tackle contemporary issues, Martin Amis and Ian McEwan, for example – 'The Child in Time' is a particular favourite."

This paragraph appears genuine and informed because it is specific.

Holidays and travel

Holidays and travel give you plenty of opportunities to present positive aspects of your character. Make the most of this area.

Admissions Tutors will want to know more than the fact that you have been to Greece and Spain.

Write about something that you did on that trip – something educational, relevant to your chosen course or that reveals something about you.

be specific

Be precise about the region you visited and be specific about your experience.

> "In the Pyrenees, I discovered the challenge of rock climbing…"

always keep your chosen course in mind

If possible, relate your subject matter to the course that you are applying for. For example, if you were applying for History, Geography or Theology, you could write:

> "In Rhodes, I was struck by the vast defences of the medieval town – and by the collision of Christian and Islamic cultures."

Hobbies and activities

Your hobbies and activities reveal a lot about your skills, motivation and application. Remember:

always keep your chosen course in mind

Interesting activities range from visiting concerts or the theatre; hobbies might include painting, mechanics, gardening or dancing. As always, be specific.

- What specific hobby do you want to cover?

- What specific skill has it developed?

- Why do you enjoy it?

Once you've fixed the area you're going to write about find something specific to say about it. If your hobby is reading plays, ask yourself:

- What type of plays? Tragedy? Comedy? Contemporary?

- Which playwrights?

- What is it about these specific writers that appeals?

Look at how the following example draws out particular qualities:

> "In my Lower Sixth, I directed 'A Midsummer Night's Dream' … a play that I desperately wanted to know intimately – beyond the restraints and rigours of academic study – to see how it worked on stage. This experience was certainly the singularly most satisfying moment in my education so far. I feel that I came of age directing that play. Not only was it intellectually and artistically challenging: working with thirty other people towards a final aim I learned a great deal about patience and tolerance in those months."

Sport

Remember that universities offer a vast range of sporting opportunities. Some universities pride themselves on developing national and international sportsmen and women.

Not everyone is interested in sport, however. Separate advice appears at the end of this section for those who want to use this space to discuss other aspects of their personality. You should still read this section to gain an understanding of the kind of information to include here.

To reach a distinguished level in any sport demonstrates **endeavour**, **commitment** and **maturity**. If you have considerable sporting ability, capitalise on this important facet of your talent and personality.

Even if you simply appreciate sport and physical fitness for its own sake, you should still let the Admissions Tutor know that you are a student who will take an active part in university life.

Depending on your experiences, your paragraph on sport might be something like this (these examples highlight the key qualities but, remember, don't use bold for emphasis in your statement):

> "As a regular member of the school hockey team I am keen to pursue this interest at university. I played centre forward in the squad that won the County Trophy. Team sports such as netball and volleyball are also particularly enjoyable. I have developed a number of abilities playing sport: being **part of a team**, **listening** and learning from others, and **helping others** in a supportive way. "

Make the section as specific to yourself as possible. The paragraph below is written by a successful school sportsman.

> "Rugby and an active social life have been carefully balanced with academic studies throughout school. I have captained my school rugby team and also the junior sections of West Hartlepool RFC. In addition I have played representative rugby for Durham County, the North of England and for the last two seasons have been in the ESRFU's Club England. Rugby has made me acutely aware of the **importance of team spirit** and **positive management.**"

This applicant successfully applied to the highly competitive course of Economics and Management at Oxford: see how he links his sporting successes to his chosen degree.

always keep your chosen course in mind

The applicant also demonstrates that he has taken sport beyond the boundaries of the school playing field. It is always a good idea to demonstrate that you pursue your interests outside the school gates.

Follow the basic process:

- List your active sporting interests – not those you watch but those in which you take part.

- Provide details about your involvement in the sport – success in competitions, training courses, tuition received, county honours, membership of clubs outside school, sponsorship, position of responsibility (e.g. team captain).

- State what you have learnt from being involved in your sporting areas – keeping your course in mind.

If you follow this advice you should end up with something like this.

> "I have played in midfield for a local football team for many years now and this year had the honour of being selected as their captain. We went on to win the County Cup for the first time in our history. And, whilst I discovered the true meaning of teamwork, I also discovered my own previously hidden talents for leadership through example, commitment and dedication."

Notice how the applicant praises himself without sounding overly arrogant. Phrases such as *"…discovered my own previously hidden talents for…"* allow you to assume a modest tone whilst at the same time demonstrating success and describing personal qualities that might otherwise sound arrogant.

Voluntary work and other activities

Sporting ability or interest is not the Admissions Tutor's primary concern. If you are not sporty, then simply don't mention it. However, you might still like to read the section dealing with sport as it will give you guidelines on how to present other activities.

Other activities can demonstrate the depth of your personality.

The Duke of Edinburgh Award is useful.

> "The Gold Duke of Edinburgh award has given me the opportunity to **take on many new challenges**; the practice and assessed expeditions frequently placing me in **demanding situations** and allowing me to deal with **unusual predicaments and work with a wide variety of people**."

Such activities as Red Cross work or voluntary service demonstrate your maturity and contribution to life outside school.

> "I am also a trained first-aider and do voluntary work for the Red Cross. When on duty I meet a wide range of different people and often have to act calmly whatever the situation."

> "I have been assisting a teacher at a local primary school for the past six months. Helping special needs children in particular has confirmed that I am patient and sensitive and has raised my interpersonal skills towards the standards shown to me by the doctors and nurses I worked with on my placements."

Section 5: Conclusion

The principal aim of your conclusion is to remind the Admissions Tutor – and any subject professors or tutors who might read your statement – that the study of your chosen course is your prime objective.

always keep your chosen course in mind

A simple yet highly effective structural device is to return the reader to the beginning of your statement.

If you can achieve this **circular structure**, it gives your statement authority and a sense of direction. It appears as though you must have known where you were heading all along.

aim for a circular structure

This method also has the advantage of returning you to your chosen course. This should be the main aim of your conclusion. Here are the opening and closing sentences of a statement.

OPENING – SECTION 1

> "When I was fourteen, I witnessed my first operation: a sarcoid removal. Since that day, I endeavoured to experience veterinary practice as often as possible."

CONCLUSION – SECTION 5

> "I believe, without doubt, the veterinary profession is for me. And I look forward to the day that I perform my first professional sarcoid removal."

Another method is to **construct a bridge** from your Section 4 that will return you to where you started: your chosen course.

construct bridges

END OF SECTION 4:

> "My main sporting interest is now golf. I have won two competitions and represent the club junior team. I have got my handicap down to single figures and have recently been selected for Durham County coaching."

CONCLUSION – SECTION 5:

> "A career option, which I would very much enjoy, would be to combine my interest in golf and **Geology** as a consultant for golf course design."

This example also suggests another method: to bridge your personal experience and your chosen course via your ambitions.

Alternatively, think of an experience that you have not already mentioned that relates to your chosen course.

You might also consider demonstrating that you are somebody who can not only survive the rigours of your chosen course but also cope with a significant event.

As stated earlier, leaving home is a rite of passage: Admissions Tutors like to see that you possess the necessary maturity for this life-changing moment.

You might say something like:

> "The diversity of my interests and range of my activities introduced me to the wider adult world. I am eager to meet new

friends, explore a new city and above all immerse myself in the study of Fine Art."

Notice that all of these conclusions have an air of finality. There is a sense that the reader has not merely reached the end of a page but the end of an argument.

Such a conclusion gives the Admissions Tutor the impression that you are in control.

Once your conclusion is written you have completed the first draft of your statement.

The five-section structure: checklist

Your five-section structure should now clearly demonstrate:

1 Why...

Why you have chosen this course.

2 What...

What you have done to demonstrate your passionate interest in the subject.

3 Academic...

That you have related your chosen course to your studies – your AS and A2 subjects.

4 Interests – activities and sport...

That you have related some areas of your activities to your chosen subject.

5 Conclusion...

That your conclusion is linked to the course via personal experience or ambition.

Redrafting: The best words in the best order

Having followed the five-part structure you now have five sections that are specifically relevant to your chosen course.

Your statement has a sense of authority, direction and purpose.

Also, because you have been specific, it possesses the all-important sense of your identity

You have done the hard work. Now you will need persistence and patience.

Far too many candidates get to this stage and consider the job done. You are *halfway* there – nearly ready for the essential redrafting process.

The statement contains most of the information that you want to communicate to the Admissions Tutor: but have you used the best words in the best order?

The purpose of your second draft is to build on your statement's structural foundations. You are aiming for a statement that is easy to read and professional.

leave for a couple of days before redrafting

However, before you begin the second draft, leave the statement for a couple of days. You will return to the statement refreshed and with a more objective eye.

It is often easier to see weaknesses and identify possible improvements when you have a clear head and a fresh start.

Useful phrases

Now that you have completed the first draft of your statement, you should reconsider the fluency of your writing.

Try to get a fluency and sense of direction in the statement. Create bridges between the section areas and paragraphs.

To help your statement read more fluently you might want to use some of the phrases below.

Such phrases help your argument flow. They give your statement that crucial sense of direction and control.

AS WELL AS...

> "**As well as** my rugby successes, I am also a competitive squash player."

BESIDES...

> "**Besides** my involvement with sports, I am also an enthusiastic actor."

HAVING...

> "**Having** taught at the local riding centre, I have…"

IN ADDITION TO...

> "**In addition to** my work experience, I have been involved in voluntary work."

NOT ONLY...BUT ALSO...

> "Not only did this allow me to…, but also to…"

You can also use such bridging phrases to move between sentences.

...MORE RECENTLY...

"Although I have been a member of the school orchestra for many years, **more recently**, I have decided to learn to play the piano."

...NOT TO MENTION...

"Being involved in the voluntary work programme, **not to mention** my work experience, has provided an opportunity to work with a diverse range of people."

...ENABLED ME...

"The opportunity to play in the school football team **enabled me** to work as part of a team."

...OPPORTUNITY TO...

"The **opportunity to** work with people was provided by my work experience."

...PROVIDED ME...

"My work experience **provided me** with an opportunity to work with a range of people."

...REINFORCED...

"My involvement in the school voluntary programme **reinforced** my decision to study a degree in Nursing."

...STRENGTHENED...

"My decision to study a degree in Economics has been **strengthened** by my enjoyment and success in my A-level course."

Avoid passive writing

Though the sentences above are reasonable, there are words and phrases that don't add much to the statement and make it rather pedestrian. They are fatty words. They serve no purpose and should be cut where possible.

avoid passive writing

Rewrite sentences that use 'has been' or 'was'.

BEFORE:

> "The **opportunity to** work with people **was** provided by my work experience."

REDRAFT:

> "My work experience provided me with the opportunity to work with people."

BEFORE:

> "My decision to study a degree in Economics **has been** strengthened by my enjoyment and success in my A-level course."

REDRAFT:

> "My decision to study a degree in Economics strengthened due to my enjoyment and success in my A-level course."

Such apparently minor alterations will make the second draft far more successful than the first. They make your second draft leaner and fitter. You will immediately sound more confident and authoritative.

Be patient and try to apply these rules of thumb where possible.

"I... I... I"

You are writing about yourself. You are the subject of the statement. Inevitably, many of your sentences will begin with 'I'.

However, it is important to give the reader a little variety: such repetition can become monotonous and there is a real danger of the reader switching off.

We have already looked at the opening and conclusion of a statement for Veterinary Science. You will find the complete statement in the examples at the end of the book on page 74.

This applicant has an impressive amount of specific information and experience to communicate. He found it difficult to avoid continually writing "I did this…" or "I did that…".

His first draft was in danger of sounding like a list of points rather than a continuous piece of writing with a sense of development and direction.

Below are his original sentences followed by his second draft variations:

ORIGINAL:

"I improved my communication skills when working and teaching at the local riding centre."

REDRAFT:

"Having taught at the local riding centre, I developed my people skills and consider myself an effective communicator."

Here he changes the sentence order replacing the first half of the sentence with the second and beginning – *"Having…"*.

In the next example, again, he puts the second half of the sentence first.

ORIGINAL:

"I witnessed my first sarcoid removal when I was fourteen."

REDRAFT:

"When I was fourteen, I witnessed my first operation: a sarcoid removal."

A similar effect can be created by using one of the useful phrases.

"**Since that day**, I have endeavoured to experience veterinary practice as much as possible."

"**As well as being** an enthusiastic tennis player, I also play squash and volleyball for the college."

"**More recently**, I decided to learn how to play the piano."

In the following examples, he doesn't lose the personal 'I' completely, but he does avoid the monotony of beginning every sentence with 'I'.

In the first, he changes the subject of the sentence to *"The challenge and discipline of science"* and ends with *"appeal to me"*. He makes himself the object of the sentence rather than its subject.

ORIGINAL:

> "I love the challenge and discipline of science…"

REDRAFT:

> "The challenge and discipline of science appeal to me."

ORIGINAL:

> "I spent many weeks over the last two years shadowing a vet."

REDRAFT:

> "Whilst spending numerous weeks in mixed practice, I had the honour of shadowing a local vet."

By introducing such variety, you can save the short statement sentence that begins with 'I' for moments of particular emphasis.

> "I consider myself confident, intelligent and sharp."

Here are some more ways of avoiding I, I, I… .

'I' at the beginning:

I enjoy rock climbing.

I am captain of the netball team.

I organised fund raising events

I enjoy sport.

I gained a number of skills from…

'I' at half way:

Rock climbing is important to me because I…

Being captain of the netball team, I…

Organising fund raising events allowed me to…

Having enjoyed playing basketball, I…

The skills I gained from…

Rather than just stating the experience itself, notice that the redraft encourages you to write about something that you learned from your experience.

Punctuation

Punctuation may seem like a relatively minor part of your statement.

However, as with paragraphing, carefully considered punctuation facilitates the reading of your statement.

It also demonstrates that you are a well-educated student: such things matter to you. It creates a good impression.

For courses where essay-writing skills are fundamental – English Literature and History, for example – paragraphing, syntax and punctuation are demonstrations of these skills.

use a variety of punctuation

Colon: use a colon in your statement:

> "I realised what I love about literature: the placing of a magnifying glass on a state of mind."

See how you could use the word 'namely' where the colon appears. This should help you decide where to use one.

> "I have developed a number of abilities playing sport: being part of a team, listening and learning from others, and helping others in a supportive way."

> "Having been entertained by Boris Johnson's ultimately shallow speech, it was Patrick Minford who provoked the most thought: Minford proved theoretically that taxation in the economy can be cut by £50 billion."

Semi-colon: use semi-colons:

> "My current original research project is a study of a quarry face section of the Cleveland Dyke near my home; I am also

investigating the alignment of phenocrysts and the degree of metamorphism in the host rocks – mainly shale."

See how the semi-colon is used to join two sentences that share a similar theme. Here's another example:

"As such my A-level studies have complemented each other; learning about European Fascism, I can better understand how those subjected to it felt."

Dash: use a dash or dashes on at least one occasion:

"I realised what I love about literature: the placing of a magnifying glass on a state of mind – the sharing of personal experience with a reader."

In the example above, what follows is a phrase – an afterthought.

You can also use dashes to add extra impact to your sentence:

"It was when I became intellectually curious – intrigued by the manner of rock formation – that my obsession with Geology really began."

Exclamation mark: use sparingly to maximise the impact:

"My coursework involved a study of faulting and folding; faulting at Staithes on the North Yorkshire coast and folding at Apes Tor in the Peak District – Geology takes you to such great places!"

An exclamation mark is a particularly effective way of establishing a slight change in tone to your statement. It puts that little bit more of your identity into your statement.

"It was amazing how much information could be extracted from an X-ray – and how tiny some of the clues were!"

"In Kowloon flea market, everything could be bought: dead dogs lie in the gutter and live chickens are decapitated to order!"

Don't overuse exclamation marks. You risk sounding breathless and unprofessional. They are effective if used sparingly.

Similarly, don't tell jokes in your statement. However, lightening the tone of the statement can help. It contributes to variety and makes the statement a more pleasurable read.

> "Having worked in my dad's betting shop for four years, I thoroughly endorse his argument that betting tax is both unfair, uneconomical and could easily be abolished!"

stick to what you know

All these uses of punctuation make for a more effective statement. **However, if you are unsure how to use them, don't use them.**

Paragraphing

If you have followed the five-section structure then your first draft is likely to have five paragraphs. Now you need to think of your paragraphs as punctuation. The purpose of paragraphing is the same as punctuation: to make your statement as easy to read as possible.

When you read your statement, you might think that one or two paragraphs are too long. This is most likely to be true of Section 2 and Section 3. Don't be afraid of dividing these sections into shorter paragraphs.

Consider the look of the statement on the page. Large blocks of text are imposing and a chore for the reader. Divide them if you can.

The same is true for paragraphs as it is for sentences: vary them.

Syntax or sentence structure

Vary sentence length. Use a range of sentence length to make things more interesting for the reader.

Short, emphatic sentences at the end of paragraphs can be particularly effective.

Spelling

It is absolutely essential that you check your statement for spelling mistakes. Use your computer spell check, but make sure you avoid American spelling.

When you have redrafted your statement, consider it again and check that you have followed the rules of thumb. Tick them off as you identify them.

- be specific

- start early

- start by using 5 sections

- be enthusiastic

- tell them something about you

- avoid obvious statement and cliché

- imply rather than state

- redraft

- prepare for interview

- show your subject means something beyond the classroom

- demonstrate maturity

- always keep your chosen course in mind

- end sentences and paragraphs with nouns

- don't ignore out of school or college activities

- aim for a circular structure

- construct bridges

- leave for a couple of days before redrafting

- avoid passive writing

- use a variety of punctuation

- stick to what you know

- include your own ideas

Who else should read it?

As you re-read and re-apply the rules of thumb, you are in effect producing the third and fourth drafts of your statement.

Keep tweaking and polishing. Once you are happy with it, and not before, give it to someone else to read.

You might begin by giving it to a member of your family.

Older brothers and sisters tend to be good readers. Many have been through the process themselves and will spot weaknesses and make suggestions for improvement.

Ask your parents to read it: but don't let them rewrite it for you. It is very obvious when a statement is written by someone else.

Ask your readers to look for the following in your statement:

- Enthusiasm for your chosen course

- Academic curiosity

- A well-rounded personality

- An attractive personality

- Maturity

Your readers should be looking to help you add these qualities if they are not already evident.

Once you have allowed people close to you to read your statement and listened to their recommendations, then you are probably ready to let your subject teacher read it.

Your subject teachers' advice will be particularly useful for Section 2. Make sure you listen to them at this point. They go through this process every year and can draw on valuable experience.

Don't be precious. There may be a sentence that you love and everyone else hates: if everyone else hates it, or most people hate it – then cut it. ***Don't dig your heels in and refuse to make changes.***

Finally – and very important – do not restrict yourself to the suggestions made in this book.

The purpose of this guide is to enable you to demonstrate what makes you tick. Admissions Tutors do not want to see everyone's statement the same.

If you read the examples of statements that follow over the next few pages, you will find that whilst they follow the same basic principles – the rules of thumb – they are not identical statements.

This is the significance of the golden rule – be specific. If you have followed the golden rule, then your personal identity must be evident in your Personal Statement.

When do I know that I have finished?

If you have been organised and worked steadily – and balanced your school work and other commitments – the entire process should have taken you three weeks or a little more.

You will see things more clearly with fresh eyes.

Once you can identify no further improvements – no matter how small:

Cut and paste your Word document into the UCAS electronic site. Follow their instructions for submission. And keep a copy of your final version in case you are called for interview

Important dates

These dates are guidelines. Always check the UCAS website in the year that you apply - www.ucas.com.

UK and EU students

1 SEPTEMBER

Annual opening date for UCAS to receive applications.

15 JANUARY

Final date for UCAS to receive applications.

15 OCTOBER

Closing date for applications to Oxford and Cambridge and many Medicine, Dentistry and Veterinary Medicine/Science courses.

1 JANUARY

First date UCAS accepts Art and Design Route B applications.

Art and Design Route B should reach UCAS between 1 January and 24 March – but UCAS advises applicants to send them by **7 March** if possible.

18 AUGUST

Start of UCAS clearing.

International students

International students who live outside the European Union can apply at any time between 1 September and 30 June.

If a student is applying from outside the EU and already has the right qualifications, he or she can apply at any time. However, please remember that most UK students will apply before 15 January and some courses may not be available after this date.

University-commended statements

All the applicants whose statements are reproduced here received offers from their first choice university.

Though some are better than others, they are all here as very good or excellent examples. Do not be overawed by them. Remember that they have been through many drafts to get to this stage.

The applicants have all used the same original five-section structure and rules of thumb. They were also, without exception, patient – and determined to achieve the very best statement.

Some technical advice

Remember that the UCAS online application does not allow you to use bold or italics. Similarly, there is little point in selecting a particular font as the electronic system ensures that all statements appear in an identical font. It is best to draft your statement in size 12 using an unfussy, efficient font, such as Verdana or Times New Roman.

Economics and Management

"How do banks make money?" and "Why doesn't the government just print more money?" Such were the naive but intriguing questions I asked myself throughout my early interest in Economics. Gradually, my questions matured; yet the answers inevitably led to more questions on an ever-increasing scale of difficulty. Such numerous questions and the diversity of the answers helped me to realise the vital importance of Economics. I have developed particular interest in the effectiveness of theoretical ideas as a means to predict the implications of changes in the economic environment.

In order to enhance my knowledge and understanding of this area, I attended the Adam Smith Institute Independent Seminar on the Open Society at the House of Commons. Having been entertained by Boris Johnson's ultimately shallow speech, it was Patrick Minford who provoked the most thought: Minford proved theoretically that taxation in the economy can be cut by £50 billion. Having worked in my dad's betting shop for four years, I thoroughly endorse his argument that betting tax is both unfair, uneconomical and could easily be abolished!

I was fortunate enough to make contacts at the ASI conference and this led to a week's work experience in Great Smith Street. There I studied the Chilean Pension system and was particularly interested to learn about Austrian Economics. However, these contacts with the ASI have not transformed me into a Government-hating "free marketeer", and I hope to accompany broadening theoretical study with further practical experience.

I was able to combine both my financial and mathematical interests when I was appointed financial director of our successful Young Enterprise company: R7 Enterprises. This brought me valuable experience in managing a budget and in dealing with unexpected problems within a company. My experience with Maths throughout school has been both enjoyable and challenging; I have attained four gold awards in the Maths Challenge. A varied selection of maths modules combined with a growing understanding of physics has added new dimensions to my problem-solving skills and numerical techniques.

Rugby and an active social life have been carefully balanced with academic studies throughout school. I have captained my school rugby team and also the junior sections of West Hartlepool RFC. In addition I have played representative rugby for Durham County, the North of England and for the last two seasons have been in the ESRFU's Club England. Rugby has made me acutely aware of the importance of team spirit and positive management. The Gold Duke of Edinburgh Award has given me the opportunity to take on many new challenges; the practice and assessed expeditions frequently placing me in demanding situations and allowing me to deal with unusual predicaments and work with a wide variety of people.

My position as Vice-Captain of school has allowed me to have a greater input within the school and to work regularly with the school's senior management team. I have particularly enjoyed working with adults, and am now eager to embark upon a period of intensive study in the field of Economics.

English Literature 1

Even before I could read I loved books! My parents were always reading to me and I am fortunate to have listened to thousands of hours of 'talking books'; this may have been when I first fell in love with the sound of words. However, I began to realise that literature was more than merely wonderful entertainment when I was twelve and won my school's public speaking prize for the first time. Three readings in particular stand out: 'The Love Song of J. Alfred Prufrock', which I read with friends in an ingenious choric arrangement; Hamlet's 'To be or not to be…'; and Macbeth's 'If it were done…'. Here I realised the compelling power of words on audience as much as reader – and began to consider their dramatic as well as their literary context. I now know that it is the power of words beyond the page that is my driving passion. My favourite poets demonstrate this: I love Shakespeare, Keats and Eliot, not just for their ideas but for their artistry. My two favourite poems are 'The Eve of Saint Agnes' and 'The Wasteland'.

I have particularly enjoyed the changing interpretations of the American dream in 'Gatsby', 'Catcher in the Rye' and 'The Virgin Suicides'. I enjoy exploring such traditions, associations and influences in literature. I am studying Rimbaud and Baudelaire as part of an optional study in French – exploring the parallels between the French and English Romantic movements.

In my Lower Sixth, I directed 'A Midsummer Night's Dream'. 'The Dream' is a play that I desperately wanted to know intimately – beyond the restraints and rigours of academic study – to see how it worked on stage. This experience was certainly the singularly most satisfying moment in my education so far. I feel that I came of age directing that play. Not only was it intellectually and artistically challenging; working with thirty other people I learned a great deal about patience and tolerance in those months. I introduced live music and dance as a part of the production. Music has always been very important to me and I play bass guitar and double bass in the school orchestra. I am captain of the school Debating Society and have represented the school at various Model United Nations conferences, where I have been commended as a distinguished delegate, as well as winning the school's mock European Parliament.

I am looking forward to conducting an individual study into Cortez and Montezuma at the time of the fall of the Aztec empire – an area I first discovered in 'The Royal Hunt of the Sun'. I am also studying ceramics at A-level. I love getting my hands dirty and have gained immense satisfaction from taking a piece of clay and transforming it into a finely glazed pot! The studio has provided an essential creative outlet – a relaxing change from academic study in the classroom.

I have a keen interest in film and cinema. I have written my first short film and hope to produce this over the next six months. This is an area that I would be interested in pursuing post university. I try to keep abreast of new writing and I have a special interest in the work of Sarah Kane. There is still so very much to learn. I cannot imagine anything more stimulating then three years studying literature.

English Literature 2

Philip Larkin's 'Love Songs In Age' made me realise what I love about literature: the placing of a magnifying glass on a state of mind – the sharing of personal experience with a reader; the translation from abstract feeling to words. How do we choose words? How do some words elicit more emotive responses than others?

Having been inspired by the AS syllabus, I have attempted to broaden my experience of different eras and genres of literature – from 'The Battle of Maldon' and medieval works, such as the magical 'Gawain and the Green Knight', through to a particular love of 20th Century literature. Orwell's belief in using "as many words from the Anglo-Saxon, and as few from the Latin as possible" is a fascinating contrast to the more cerebral T. S. Eliot. Orwell wants nothing to distract from his purpose, whilst Eliot's deliberate difficulty rewards the reader with an eventual blinding clarity.

To me there is much more to English than just its writing: the social and historical contexts of 'Animal Farm' or non-fiction such as 'Down and Out in Paris and London' provide individual perspectives to my understanding of History and Politics. As such my A-level studies have complemented each other; reading about European Fascism, I can better understand how those subjected to it felt.

Debating has offered an enjoyable, and successful, sideline to my studies: in my Comprehensive School against 6th Form opposition, I won both the national "Motorola Youth Parliament" competition and the regional heat of the European Parliament competition. More recently I have enjoyed the Cambridge Union format, testing my intellectual dexterity and a skill for improvisation – something I look forward to continuing. These skills have been further tested in my positions as Chair of School and Sixth Form Councils, as has the role of School Prefect and sporting captain.

Playing percussion to grade 8 standard, I play in school, county and jazz orchestras, teach percussion and play saxophone to a grade 6 standard and enjoy professional show work. A performance of 'Cabaret' led me to read Isherwood's 'Berlin Novels', introducing me to a disarmingly honest portrayal of a political situation. I also acted in a production of 'Animal Farm', finding the Brechtian interpretation of Orwell's allegory to be a new and invigorating representation.

Work experience as a sports reporter for a local paper gave me a taste of a future journalistic career. I am inspired by A. A. Gill's turn of phrase and eye for controversy and Paul Hayward's distinct and engaging style of sports writing. I, too, have a complementary love of sport, and have represented school and district at football; school, district and county at rugby and cricket and enjoy cycling, water sports and skiing.

I have had many enriching opportunities to travel, including trips to South America, China and Russia. I found it fascinating to be illiterate for the duration, shedding new light on Pinter's 'Mountain Language' and the attempt to control people by controlling their language. I have no doubt where my interests lie. Language, to me, is identity, and I look forward to the opportunity of immersing myself further in English.

Geology

Even before I fully understood what they were, rocks, minerals, fossils and gemstones had a compelling fascination. I was attracted by their vivid colours and amazed by the ages of the specimens that I found and bought. But it was when I became intellectually curious – intrigued by the manner of their formation – that my obsession with Geology really began.

My early interest in Geology was fuelled by reading 'Down to Earth', and I became an obsessive collector of the 'Treasures of the Earth' series over its three-year period. When I was fourteen I attended 'Scottish Geology Week', a fascinating five days of geological discovery; an inspection of Arthur's Seat; a visit to the BGS in Edinburgh; a view of the cretaceous-tertiary boundary; and a quest for Grapholites in Dobbs Lynn were highlights of a totally compelling five days.

As my secondary school did not offer Geology GCSE, I found a private tutor and we had two great years of one-to-one study. My coursework involved a study of faulting and folding; faulting at Staithes on the North Yorkshire coast and folding at Apes Tor in the Peak District – Geology takes you to such great places! My laboratory experiment investigated the different effects of acid rain on limestone and granite.

'Rock shops' have always lured me, and I have collected a wide variety of specimens. My current pride and joy is a section of a Brazilian Geode with spectacular amethyst crystals – closely followed by my precious malachite and onyx chess set. I have been a keen lapidarist since primary school and have a full range of equipment. My favourite labour of love is my large cross-sectioned ammonite with dog-tooth calcite crystals in all of its chambers.

My current original research project is a study of a quarry face section of the Cleveland Dyke near my home; I am also investigating the alignment of phenocrysts and the degree of metamorphism in the host rocks – mainly shale. I also intend to return to Staithes and complete my study on faulting.

Geology is my passion. I simply could not consider studying anything but Geology at university.

I enjoyed completing my Bronze D of E and gaining a First Aid qualification. For the Service qualification of my Gold Award I am assisting the staff team in a Special Needs School. I feel I have learnt a great deal from this, in self-confidence, personal skills and working in a team situation. I also enjoyed playing an active role as part of a team helping to run the OAPs' Christmas party at my College.

I have received four awards in National Mathematics Competitions, of which the best was a Silver Certificate in the British Intermediate Mathematics Contest. While at school I played in various team sports, e.g. Hockey, Football, Rugby and Cricket, however my main sporting interest is now golf. I have won two competitions and represent the club junior team. I have got my handicap down to single figures and have recently been selected for Durham County coaching.

A career option, which I would very much enjoy, would be to combine my interest in golf and Geology as a consultant for golf course design.

Medicine

In my opinion no other occupation has so much to offer as medicine. The challenge of learning complex anatomy and physiology and ultimately specialising in a particular field such as cardiology excite me immensely.

To help me gain insight into the world of medicine, I spent three weeks on work experience placements during the summer holidays. I worked in the Accident and Emergency Department in North Tees Hospital, in the Intensive Care Unit at Middlesbrough General and in a General Practitioners' Surgery in Thornaby. At the A&E Department, I observed nurses performing triage and how they extracted vital information about a patient's history. I shadowed doctors into treatment rooms, observed a variety of interesting lacerations and fractures and witnessed the removal of several foreign bodies! I particularly enjoyed looking at X-rays as the doctor would explain what they were looking for and what the X-ray showed. It was amazing how much information could be extracted from an X-ray – and how tiny some of the clues were!

The Intensive Care Unit showed me a very different side of medicine. I observed a tracheostomy and a muscle biopsy. I was privileged to join the ward rounds each morning and worked closely with the consultant anaesthetist who explained how the life maintaining equipment operated and how each patient was being treated. Working at the Medical Centre showed me how vital team work is to the profession. The GP I shadowed at the surgery also worked at the hospital, and I was able to observe him performing colonoscopies and gastroscopies as well as the removal of various cysts and ulcers.

I enjoy studying the A levels I am taking and have achieved a high standard of work throughout my course. I maintain a good working relationship with my tutors. Studying Maths enabled me to develop a logical way of thinking which is required by medicine, whilst Chemistry has given me a firm foundation on which to build the physiology I will learn at medical school. In Physics, at the moment, I am studying the electron, which I find fascinating. The problem solving nature of all my subjects should stand me in good stead for the many varied and taxing challenges I will face once I embark on a medical career.

I lead a very active life outside of college playing a diverse range of sports. My favourite team game is hockey where I represent the North East of England. Gold Duke of Edinburgh increased my love of the outdoors; I have become a proficient rock climber, mountaineer and skier. I captained my school hockey, cricket and rugby teams, enhancing my ability to work under pressure, communicate effectively and work in a team. I am very fond of music in all its forms and regularly play the piano and guitar in a band.

I have been assisting a teacher at a local primary school for the past six months. Helping special needs children in particular has confirmed that I am patient and sensitive and has raised my interpersonal skills towards the standards shown to me by the doctors and nurses I worked with on my placements. I am looking forward to the intellectual demands of medical school and the day when I assess and diagnose my first patient.

Psychology

My decision to study psychology at advanced level was influenced by my fascination with the theories and explanations behind human and animal behaviour. From an early age, I was aware that adults responded to boys and girls according to their gender. And later, when travelling to countries such as South Africa and the Arab Emirates, I was further intrigued by the behavioural, perceptual and cognitive differences between people of different cultures.

I am particularly interested in the links between physiological and neurological systems and behaviour, for example, how reduced levels of serotonin contribute to the onset of seasonal affective disorder. Studying biology alongside psychology has allowed me to understand many of these links. I have thoroughly enjoyed studying case studies such as 'Lateralisation of Brain Function' by Sperry and 'The cognitive, social and psychological determinants of emotion' by Scacter and Singer. Such work made me determined to pursue psychology at university and beyond.

'Psychopathology' by John D. Stirling and S. E. Hellewell, 'The Physiological Basis of Behaviour' by Kevin Sibler and 'Mind Watching – Why we Behave the Way we Do' by Hans and Michael Eysenk helped me gain a deeper understanding of topics such as mental illness. These books made me aware of the significance of diagnostic labels, particularly when they cause people to systematically re-interpret all aspects of a patient's behaviour as symptomatic of the disorder they have been labelled with. Having read these books I became aware of the significance of diagnostic labels, particularly when they cause people to systematically re-interpret all aspects of a patient's behaviour as symptomatic of the disorder they have been labelled with.

My involvement in many, varied extra curricular activities has given me the valuable opportunity to develop important social skills. Having completed my Bronze Duke of Edinburgh Award, I am currently working towards finishing the Gold Award. In participating in this award scheme, I learned the value of teamwork, improvisation and perhaps above all, determination and self-belief. It has also given me an opportunity to enjoy helping the local community as I have become involved in fundraising for the Butterwick Hospice and a paired readership scheme. I have a keen interest in sport and enjoy representing my College in netball, hockey and tennis. I hope to pursue my interest in sport at university.

Perhaps the most challenging and rewarding aspect of my extra curricular activities in college is my role as Vice Captain. This position has given me the opportunity to develop my leadership and inter-personal skills as it involves dealing with pupils of all ages and needs. Balancing responsibilities such as the day to day running of the school with 4 A levels and various extra curricular activities made me intensely aware of prioritising time management and self discipline. Looking towards the future, I am extremely excited by the prospect of a career in the field of neuropsychology, an area that is flourishing with fresh discoveries, technological advances and knowledge.

Tourism

I consider relating well to people to be my strongest quality. Following my experience of working in an exclusive 4* hotel and an inner city fish and chip café, I have discovered my ability to socially interact with people of varying social and ethnic backgrounds and of all ages. This trait has encouraged me to pursue a career path where I can continue to encounter a diversity of people.

I have a great interest in travel. My excursions have included participating in the Middlesbrough / Oberhausen peace link exchange, an archaeological tour of Rome and Pompeii, skiing in Vermont and a package tour to Crete with a friend. I feel I would succeed at and benefit from studying a degree in hospitality and tourism management. This would give me the opportunity to use and develop my communication skills and also provide me with the chance to travel.

I am highly organised and reliable and have succeeded in organising successful charity events – selling 300 toasties in just 5 hours! I am always keen to get involved in school life by helping out with different schemes and events. One of these was the paired reading scheme where we were each assigned a younger child who we took under our wing and read with once or twice a week, recording progress. I have also been a valued member of the girls' hockey team and have never been shy to read in assemblies and church services. My heavy involvement in school life resulted in me being awarded a prefectship. This has given me the opportunities to develop my leadership skills.

I have considerable experience of communicating with people. In my work experience I have worked in a residential home. I am also a trained first-aider and do voluntary work for the Red Cross. When on duty I meet a wide range of different people and often have to act calmly whatever the situation.

While studying for my A levels I have succeeded in improving my confidence and public speaking skills from my Theatre Studies course. I have also developed the ability to interact with people in other European countries by gaining my German AS. I hope to continue improving my German while studying my chosen course.

I work well in a team and have had occasions to benefit from these skills when completing my Gold Duke of Edinburgh's expedition and when acting in numerous plays in and out of school. I enjoy challenges and find them rewarding and enjoyable. I am a member of Cliffe Theatre, which consists of members mostly older than myself. Here I have contributed by performing in many productions, my latest being the part of Catherine in Terence Ratigan's "The Winslow Boy". When not on stage I enjoy helping in front of house by selling programmes and serving refreshments. Other hobbies include regularly attendance of a gym and playing the piano.

I look forward to the challenge of working in one of the fastest developing global industries and feel that I have the ambition and drive to succeed.

Travel and tourism

Understanding the cultures and behaviour of people from all over the world and observing the reception some countries have towards other nationalities intrigues me. On a recent visit to Kai Tak and Lap Kok in Hong Kong, I was captivated by its diversity and contrasts. In Kowloon flea market everything could be bought: dead dogs lie in the gutter and live chickens are decapitated to order! Turn a corner and you are in a bustling modern capital surrounded by sports cars and up-market boutiques. I loved the contrast and this moment sums up my interest in Travel and Tourism.

I feel that all three of my A-level subjects complement my choice of degree through the understanding of people, the communication with foreigners and the understanding of the world and its settlement patterns.

I feel that this course would be suited to me as I enjoy working with a variety of people and nationalities and I have a strong interest in the travel industry. In the summer following my GCSEs, I organised my own work experience at Teesside International Airport where I was situated in every department in the airport over the space of a week. The most fascinating was observing the staff at British Midland. This included customer services, load controlling, boarding and dispatching the aircraft to London Heathrow.

Outside of school, I have developed a keen interest in flying and I have been lucky enough to have one of the lessons at the American Flyers club in Fort Lauderdale! Additional work experience includes being a part-time sales assistant in a local supermarket and waitress in a Thai restaurant. All of these positions either held or hold an amount of responsibility and enabled me to work with and for a wide range of people.

In addition to flying, I am very keen on all sports, in particular hockey. I have represented all of my schools as well as my district, County and the North of England. I was fortunate to captain the U-14 and U-16 district and county teams. A new interest in my life is extreme sports. Having white water rafted in Australia, I decided to take up the challenge of an 11,000ft skydive over Durham and raised just over £600 for Mind. I also completed an ill-fated Bungee jump in aid of the Owen Swift appeal which found me hanging 180ft by my left arm above a pub car park! I find time to relax with my friends by going to the cinema, going out for meals or by listening to a wide variety of music.

Within school I have reached school prefect status, and last July I was appointed vice-captain of my house. This position of responsibility will allow me to share new ideas with the group and to display a degree of leadership skills to ensure the smooth running of the group. These skills were also needed when I completed the bronze stage of the Duke of Edinburgh Award. I look forward to being able to continue these interests and hobbies when I reach university.

Veterinary Science

When I was fourteen, I witnessed my first operation: a sarcoid removal. Since that day, I endeavoured to experience veterinary practice as often as possible. Whilst spending numerous weeks in the past two years in mixed practice, I shadowed a highly respected local vet, and had many experiences with large animal surgery, particularly equine – my specific interest.

During my time watching equine practice, I realised the pragmatic necessity for shoe removal and other more practical tasks such as dorsal wall resection. Consequently, I spent a week with a farrier learning to remove shoes and further investigating the anatomy of the foot. I enjoyed such hands-on understanding and therefore spent a week at a local practice specialising in dairy work and a further week at a dairy farm, striking up a friendship with an affable Friesian bull calf! My respect for animals grew.

I attended two residential courses at the University of Nottingham, 'VetSix' and 'VetSim': sessions ranged from reptiles and exotics to suturing, keyhole surgery and emergency callout simulation, and I attended lectures on parasites, surgical techniques and holistic treatments. I found both courses intriguing and their diversity affirmed my desire to be a vet. The challenge and discipline of science and the rewards of helping animals wherever possible appeal to me. I do, on the contrary, understand the occasional need to end life, and consequently spent a challenging day in an abattoir.

I've found my A-level choices highly gratifying and relevant to the pursuit of my career. I enjoy anatomical studies in Biology; Physics helped me understand infinitesimal concepts and Maths taught me to consider problems rationally and apply correct procedure – an area that might help in future diagnoses. I sincerely enjoy studying: my academic rigour, enthusiasm and healthy level of perfectionism led to highly gratifying AS level results.

I am currently approaching the end of my second season with British Eventing, competing at both pre-novice and novice level. I thoroughly enjoy riding and competing in my spare time. I have ridden all my life and consequently learnt much about animal husbandry and behaviour. Due to their intelligence, I find horses the most intriguing and rewarding of creatures. Having taught at the local riding centre, I developed my people skills and consider myself an effective communicator. Oakland Surgery complimented me on my communication skills, and I consider myself confident, intelligent and sharp.

I enjoyed completing Bronze, Silver and Gold Duke of Edinburgh's Awards and managing my Young Enterprise company. A confident public speaker, I debated numerous times in local and national competition. More recently, my appointment as Captain of School proved my confidence and ability to speak, often in front of audiences of over 500. I believe, without doubt, the veterinary profession is for me. I am enthusiastically committed to putting my passion back into my work: for me being a vet is more than a job – it is a service. And I look forward to the day that I perform my first sarcoid removal.

Notes

Notes